£4

FRANCIS PRYOR

Director, The Welland Valley Project

WITHDRAWN

FENGATE

THE
PAUL HAMLYN
LIBRARY

DONATED BY
THE PAUL HAMLYN
FOUNDATION
TO THE
BRITISH MUSEUM

opened December 2000

SHIRE ARCHAE

D0544729

2

TITLES IN THE SHIRE ARCHAEOLOGY SERIES

Cover illustration
Late neolithic (2000 BC) ring-ditch at
Fengate. This circular ditch originally enclosed
a small settlement and was later reused to
provide make-up for a barrow mound.

THE
BRITISH
MUSEUM
THE PAUL HAMLYN LIBRARY

936.
265
\
pRY

Published by
SHIRE PUBLICATIONS LTD
Cromwell House, Church Street, Princes Risborough,
Aylesbury, Bucks, HP17 9AJ, UK.

Series Editor: James Dyer

Copyright © Francis Pryor, 1982
All rights reserved.
No part of this publication may be reproduced or transmitted
in any form or by any means, electronic or mechanical,
including photocopy, recording, or any information storage and retrieval system, without
permission in writing from the publishers.

ISBN 0 85263 577 X

First published 1982

Printed in Great Britain by
C. I. Thomas & Sons (Haverfordwest) Ltd,
Press Buildings, Merlins Bridge, Haverfordwest.

Contents

List of illustrations

1
Introduction

A note on dates and periods

Most of the dates cited below are based on uncalibrated radiocarbon determinations and are quoted in very round terms. Readers wanting greater precision should consult the four published reports, especially the Fourth Report, fig. 272, which correlates radiocarbon years with calendar years, as presently understood.

The prehistoric archaeological periods used are also very generalised: neolithic 4000 to 2000 BC; earlier bronze age 2000 to 1200 BC; later bronze age 1200 to 700 BC; earlier iron age 700 to 400 BC; later iron age 400 BC to the Roman Conquest (AD 43) and after (about AD 65/70). This is further subdivided into: middle iron age 400/350 to 100 BC; late iron age 100 BC to AD 50/60.

The opportunity to excavate Fengate under modern conditions arose from the planned expansion of Peterborough New Town. Land was purchased by the New Town authorities in advance of development and adequate time for proper archaeological investigation was allowed from the outset. We are keen, therefore, to acknowledge the helpful co-operation we received, at all stages of the project, from the staff of Peterborough Development Corporation. Funds for digging and post-excavation research were provided by the Ancient Monuments Inspectorate of the Department of the Environment and the Royal Ontario Museum of Toronto, Canada, where the author was an Assistant Curator.

We will return to the recent project shortly, but first we should consider the previous research in the region. Despite its poor qualities as a builder's material, the gravel underlying Fengate has been exploited as ballast for many years. No doubt this reflects transport costs in the earlier decades of the twentieth century; today, gravel of suitable quality is mainly extracted from the Welland valley, 10 miles (16 km) north of Fengate. This area, like most gravel regions, is also extraordinarily rich in archaeological sites, of which the best known is Maxey, where there are two neolithic henges, a neolithic 'cursus' monument approximately 2 kilometres ($1\frac{1}{4}$ miles) long, a neolithic mortuary enclosure, a probable neolithic causewayed enclosure, fifty barrows (probably early bronze age) and substantial settlements of iron age, Roman, Saxon and later dates. This enormous complex of sites is currently being surveyed and excavated by the Fengate team as part of the follow-up to the work described here.

The site was discovered by a Peterborough solicitor and distinguished amateur antiquarian, the late G. Wyman Abbott, FSA. Abbott visited the various small Fengate gravel pits regularly from the early years of the twentieth century. He knew the workmen and foremen, and in the less hurried times in which he lived it was possible to discuss matters at length: he explained what to look for on the quarry face and taught the men to recognise the cruder hand-made pots that characterise the neolithic and bronze age periods. He was able, too, to produce schematised drawings of the pits that produced the original Fengate finds, and the objects themselves may now be seen, newly displayed, in the archaeological galleries of Peterborough Museum. Perhaps the best known objects recovered by Abbott were sherds of very coarsely made, highly decorated pottery belonging to the late neolithic period (centred on 2000 BC). These vessels gave the name *Peterborough* to a tradition of pottery that is found widely in Britain; *Fengate ware* is a variety within the larger style that has many points in common with earlier bronze age pottery, especially the collared urns.

It is apparent from Abbott's drawings that many of the pits were once waterlogged in their lower fillings, and this would suggest that they originally functioned as small 'sock' wells, of a type that was still in use in the twentieth century.

Abbott saw that his regularly collected material was properly labelled and he kept an important notebook, now at Cambridge, detailing the circumstances of his various discoveries. Clearly the salvage conditions under which he worked were far from ideal and it is now, unfortunately, not easy to locate his findspots with any accuracy; but he was a pioneer of rescue archaeology and deserves great credit for discovering and preserving a substantial part of this important complex of sites. He also had the true amateur archaeologist's regard for proper and prompt publication and, being a man of influence, was able to draw on the expertise of the foremost scholars of the time. People such as Reginald Smith, E. T. Leeds, Clare Fell and Christopher Hawkes, all well known authorities on British prehistory, contributed to or wrote large parts of the reports that appeared on his discoveries.

The archaeological world, and especially the Nene Valley Research Committee, which has responsibility for the Peterborough region, was disturbed when, in the later 1960s, it was decided to enlarge the population of Peterborough from 80,000 to 180,000. The new population would have to be housed and employed in a region rich in archaeological sites, of which Fengate was just one. The Committee requested a special survey into the antiquities threatened by the New

A SIMPLIFIED GEOLOGY

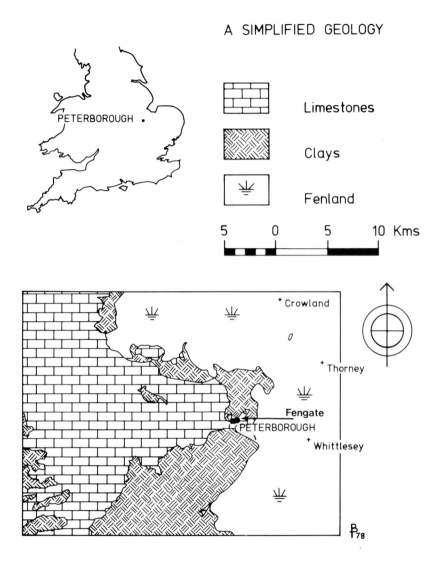

Fig. 1. Map showing the location of Fengate and a simplified geology of the region.

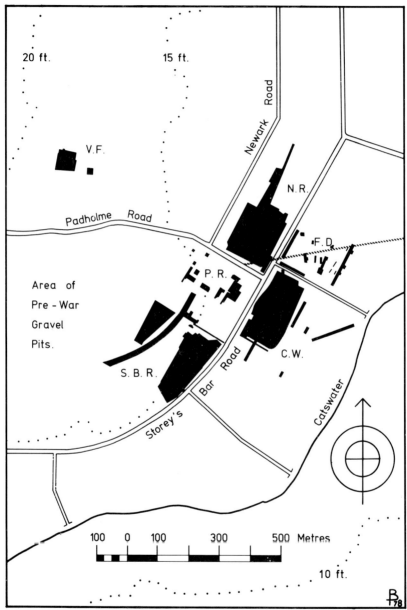

Fig. 2. Plan showing the areas excavated (in black) and the location of the subsites: CW, Cat's Water; FD, Fourth Drove; NR, Newark Road; PR, Padholme Road; SBR, Storey's Bar Road; VF, Vicarage Farm. The Fen Causeway (a Roman road) is shown by a slashed line.

Town, which was promptly produced by the Royal Commission on Historical Monuments in 1969. This survey contained a comprehensive review of all previous work at Fengate and, perhaps most important of all, it included numerous recent aerial photographs which showed that there had been considerable ancient activity far outside the well known area investigated by Abbott. There was hardly a field anywhere in Fengate, undamaged by gravel-digging or house building, that did not show clear indications of buried archaeological sites. The reader may wonder how it was possible that the aerial camera was able to penetrate below the soil to reveal the archaeology beneath, and a short explanation is necessary.

Fengate, or large parts of it, has been ploughed continuously for many years. The constant action of the plough has tended to smooth out the natural and man-made bumps on the landscape. Sharply defined features such as barrows or ditches are either so flattened that they vanish completely or else they can only be discerned when viewed in oblique sunlight from high in the air. Oblique light, in winter or during summer evenings, casts long deep shadows that exaggerate the rise and fall of the land surface. Fengate, however, had been ploughed quite flat. In cases such as this one must rely on the differential growth of cereal crops to reveal buried features. Thus the basic principles behind cropmark archaeology are quite simple.

Light, freely draining subsoils, such as sand or gravel, may be permanently affected when disturbed. If, for example, a field boundary ditch is dug it is probably maintained open, a hedge may be planted on the bank alongside it and topsoil will accumulate on its sides and bottom. The ditch subsequently passes out of use and is abandoned. Ploughing eventually levels the spot where it had once been. Below the ground there is now a long ditch-shaped deposit of hedge roots, leaves, topsoil and so on, which cannot drain as effectively as the gravel subsoil into which it has been cut. The combination of damper ground and higher, more nourishing, humic content causes vegetation directly above the buried ditch to flourish. It grows faster and more luxuriantly than crops around it; from the air these patterns of differential crop growth can be seen to form a coherent picture. In theory it is simple to understand cropmarks: in practice it may often be difficult. Natural agencies, such as frost action during the last ice age, may produce cropmarks that appear deceptively man-made. Fengate had its share of these. Genuinely man-made cropmarks may be superimposed time after time so that it is virtually impossible to untangle the mass, without recourse to large-scale excavation. At Fengate we were generally fortunate in the latter respect: people tended to occupy discreet areas at different clearly defined archaeological

Plate 1. Aerial view of cropmarks looking north-east over the Newark Road subsite, with Padholme Road crossing the foreground. The Fen Causeway shows as a pale 'negative' crop-mark. (Photograph by J. K. St Joseph, Cambridge University Collection; copyright reserved.)

Fig. 3 (opposite). Simplified plan of the main Fengate cropmarks. A, location of neolithic house; B, late neolithic settlement; 1-10, location of main second millennium BC ditches; C, Cat's Water iron age settlement.

periods. We had to undertake a complex 'unscrambling' operation only on the large Cat's Water iron age settlement, which is described in more detail below.

When it came to the interpretation of air photographs, the main problem was caused by thick accumulations of surface flood clays which were laid down in the third century AD. These poorly draining clays effectively masked buried features from the aerial camera; we would never, for instance, have discovered the large Cat's Water iron age settlement had we not had other techniques at our disposal. The settlement was revealed by a survey which analysed the varying concentrations of soil phosphate in core samples taken on a ten-metre grid. High levels of soil phosphate indicate the presence of ancient occupation; phosphate analysis will be discussed below. The survey, carried out for us by colleagues at the British Museum Research Laboratory, showed unusually high phosphates just below the flood

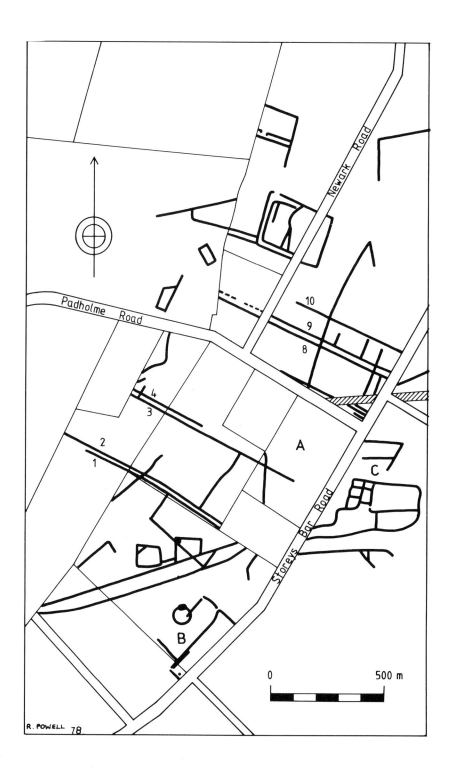

Padholme Road

Newark Road

Storeys Bar Road

10
9
8

4
3

2
1

A

B

C

0   500 m

R. POWELL 78

clays in the north-west part of the Cat's Water subsite. These results suggested that a large settlement lay hidden beneath the blanketing flood clays. We planned our subsequent soil stripping accordingly and revealed the settlement buried beneath in its entirety.

The site was enormous and it became necessary to subdivide it into various subsites, which are illustrated in fig. 2. In the first two seasons (1971 and 1972) we recorded finds in the conventional way, by layer and feature alone; by 1973 we had realised that this was not enough and thereafter recorded everything in three dimensions, in horizontal terms to the nearest square metre.

The reason for this elaborate procedure is simple. Imagine, for example, that a ditch was dug around a building to drain the run-off from the roof. The building was then abandoned and subsequently levelled by the plough, so that all that remained was the eaves-drip gully. The only archaeological evidence for that structure, and what took place in and around it, is now preserved in the gully. When people go in and out of a house they may often kick rubbish to either side of the front door; this sort of behaviour leads to clearly patterned distributions of, for example, pottery, where there may be neat groups of sherds on either side of the doorway. Other patterns may also be distinguished. Animal behaviour, on the other hand, produces different results in which patterning is less evident.

The subsites revealed a vast amount of information: there were hundreds of features, thousands of layers, tens of thousands of finds and hundreds of thousands of animal bones. All this must be planned, photographed where necessary, and recorded. From 1971 to 1973 we recorded information on blank cards which were then indexed to provide a simple cross-referenced archive. By 1974 the project was producing too much data to be handled in this way so we designed and printed a series of computer-compatible cards in which features were recorded by ticking various multiple-choice boxes. These cards proved a great success and are still in use, only slightly modified, today.

Large areas had to be cleared of topsoil and various types of machine were used to do this. Contrary to popular belief, earthmoving machines, despite their power and size, can work to very fine tolerances; we required precision to the nearest 2-3 inches (50-75 mm), as a matter of course; in certain situations we could use the machines to shave even more finely. When using machines it is vital that the topsoil be as thoroughly studied as possible before it is removed. Even if it has been ploughed for centuries, the ploughsoil still retains evidence for the 'vertical component', rubbish heaps for example, that survives so rarely on lowland sites in Britain.

2
Why Fengate?
The site in its setting

The sites at Fengate form part of an extensive spread of prehistoric and Romano-British occupation along the fringes of the western Fenlands, both north and south of Peterborough. Situated on the fringe of the Fens, ancient settlements were able to exploit two contrasting but complimentary ecological zones. It was this fen-edge location, sandwiched between true fen and upland that made the site such an attractive proposition to communities in pre-industrial times.

The Fens are a region of extraordinary archaeological potential. They are surprisingly recent and arose as a result of the melting of the enormous areas of ice which locked up so much sea water during the last great ice age. About nine thousand years ago the level of the North Sea (which barely existed as such) was some 40-50 metres (130-160 feet) lower than it is today. Conditions became gradually warmer and sea levels rose as the ice melted. Groups who subsisted on hunting and gathering, rather than farming, were able to pursue their game across the marshy plains of what is today the southern North Sea. Modern trawlers have brought early post-glacial mesolithic spearheads to the surface from the sea bed near the Leman and Ower banks, where they were covered by 35 to 40 metres (115-130 feet) of water. Other broadly contemporary finds have also been made in the southern North Sea. These finds illustrate most convincingly the slow but relentless rise of the post-glacial sea level.

Shortly before 7000 BC, rising sea levels gradually began to affect drainage further inland. As the engineer Vermuyden (who was to drain large areas of the Fens in the seventeenth century) appreciated well, land drainage depends on rivers, and they, in turn, will only function efficiently if their outfall to the sea is free from obstruction. Storm and tidal deposits along the rising coastline would have adversely affected the outfalls of the slow-running rivers flowing across the natural dip which today forms the floor of the great Fenland basin. As flow into the sea was impeded, so reed and sedge thrived and peats began to form. At first peat formation was mainly confined to low-lying wet areas, such as river channels or shallow meres. The well known prehistoric fen settlement at Shippea Hill has evidence for peat formation in a river channel at about 6500 BC. It is hard to be precise, but peats were probably forming at Holme Fen, 6 miles (10 km) south of Fengate, by 4000 BC. Huge oaks that once grew in the primeval forest that covered the Fen Basin were drowned by rising water levels. They collapsed into the mire, where they were saved from decay by waterlogging. These trees, preserved for us by nature, are being ripped out of the ground as part of the normal course of modern farming. Once peat is drained it soon dries and oxidises and in this state may be blown away. This process has caused the surface of the peat to fall dramatically. At Holme Fen, a cast iron pillar sunk into the underlying basal clay so that its top, in 1848, was level with the surface of the ground now projects 4 metres (13 feet) in the air! Most parts of the peat Fens were drained in the seventeenth and eighteenth centuries, so it is hardly surprising that preserved basal forest trees are now being struck by the plough.

In its natural undrained state the peat Fenland offered an extraordinarily rich source of food, fuel, pasture and many other necessities of life. Readers of Maisie Taylor's book *Wood in Archaeology*, also in this series (Shire Publications, 1981), will know what a variety of products can be obtained from willow, perhaps the most frequently encountered tree of the fen-edge. During wetter periods of its history the fen would have been covered with large expanses of alder, a soft wood which is easily worked and naturally resistant to decay. In addition to timber and peat for fuel, the fen provided reeds for thatching, while the large meadows around its fringes, which were kept naturally fertile by the nutrient-rich waters flowing off the surrounding drier land, yielded almost inexhaustible supplies of grass for hay and grazing. Although doubtless exploited in summer too, the waters of the Fens provided fish and fowl to augment the meagre winter fare that was the normal lot of prehistoric groups living in less fortunate circumstances.

It is therefore apparent that the Fens were not the inhospitable, trackless wastes that they sometimes seem. Their history after about 4000 BC is rich and varied: sometimes they were wet, sometimes they were comparatively dry; the salt content of their waters would vary too, depending on events nearer the coast and this would have a considerable effect on local plant and animal life. Fen-edge communities depended on the flora and fauna of the peatlands to a large extent, so they too were ultimately affected by such changes. Recent research into the archaeology and past biology of the Fens is showing how delicately nature was adjusted to this complex and rather unstable environment of extraordinary variety. The Fenland today, apart from obvious differences in soil colour (black for peats, pale brown for marine silts), looks very uniform: flat, transected by straight drains,

Plate 2. The Holme Fen post. The top of this post was level with the ground surface in 1848. Note the birch woodland growing on the fen in the background.

Plate 3. Bog oaks lying on a fen field, south of Peterborough. These once massive trees were drowned by rising water levels about six thousand years ago. They have recently been exposed by the shrinking (see plate 2) of the overlying peat soil caused by drainage and modern methods of agriculture.

hedgeless, treeless and, to some, monotonous. In antiquity it was very different: the peats were broached by numerous islands cloaked in forest, whilst wooded natural stream banks and levees would provide solid ground for scattered farmsteads, much as they do today. The stream banks, too, would allow communication across the wetlands and would be covered by different types of vegetation, depending on their age and the salinity of the waters around them.

The complexity, variability and richness of the natural resources that were offered by this environment must be fully appreciated before the ancient settlements of the fen-edge can be understood. The wetlands of the fen undoubtedly provided the chief incentive for fen-edge settlement, but another, drier, component was also necessary if the potential of the fen was to be adequately realised.

The wide, almost flat lands of river valleys which drain into the Fen Basin have been a focus for human settlement since the wetlands began to form. The well drained, light gravel soils of this region provide a safe haven from whence to exploit the Fens. As sea levels rose, so did the approximate line of seasonal flooding; thus land safe from winter floods in iron age times would not have been suitable for year-round occupation during the Saxon period. Fengate is a fine example of this type of marginal region: in neolithic times it was safe from all floods; in the bronze age it was safe from all but severe winter flooding, but by the iron age it was very marginal. Finally, by the later Roman period it could only be exploited in summer.

The gravels were well suited for the growing of crops which would not have survived in the wetlands, and they also provided limited, but assured, areas suitable for winter pasture. Water, which is so essential to the well-being of cattle, was readily obtainable less than 6 feet (1.8 m) below the surface. Unlike peat, which is unsuited for permanent settlement, gravel provides an ideal, stable and freely draining subsoil for house foundations.

Located on the flood-free gravel soils at Fengate, communities had an ideal 'home base' from which to exploit the seasonally available resources of the wetlands. The archaeological evidence makes it clear that this exploitation took place on a surprisingly large scale, and we must now look at the evidence more closely to appreciate how well ancient communities adapted to the vicissitudes and opportunities presented by their environment.

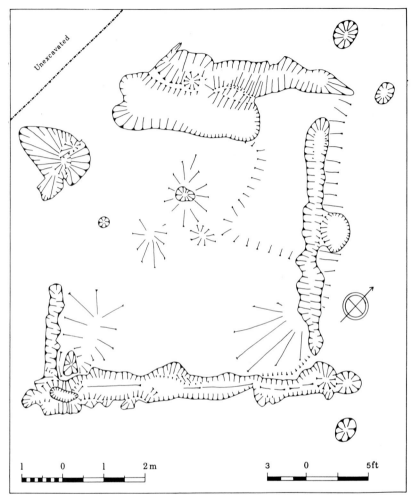

Fig. 4. Ground plan of the foundation trenches of the earlier neolithic house, Padholme Road subsite, 1972 season.

3
Phase one: consolidation

The earliest inhabitants of Fengate do not concern us here, as evidence for their existence is very sparse. They lived by fishing, hunting and gathering the plant food in the woodland and streams of the lower Nene valley. Their presence must, however, have affected their surroundings in many respects that cannot be detected using archaeological techniques alone and it is easy to underestimate their importance. The relationship of these mesolithic groups to the first communities of neolithic farmers is a matter of considerable interest, if indeed they both represent ethnically distinct populations. In many respects the actual mechanism by which farmers, or the idea of farming, spread is unimportant. What matters is that shortly after 4000 BC there is good evidence for the establishment of a way of life which was not to alter in its essentials until post-medieval times.

There is no coherent archaeological evidence for the very earliest neolithic occupation at Fengate. Settlements of this period are notoriously elusive and are particularly rare in lowland England. Today one would expect to find very early neolithic material further out in the Fens, on islands, stream banks or buried beneath the peats. Fortunately, one such site has been discovered and excavated in the southern Fens at Shippea Hill by Professor Clark and information from this important site will be used to fill out our interpretation of Fengate in its earliest phases.

We have referred to this first period as being one of consolidation since, as yet, there is no evidence for the initial pioneering phase. It is most probable that the earliest farmers carried on a way of life not unlike that of the first European 'log cabin' settlers of North America. Although actual archaeological evidence for slash-and-burn agriculture is very thin, we may assume that clearings were made in the forest cover (by whatever means), and that small plots of cereals were grown there. A few livestock would be grazed beyond the fields or gardens, either in the forest or in plots that had been cleared in previous seasons but had since been allowed to revert to scrub. This pattern of land use may frequently involve the clearing and subsequent reclearing of secondary woodland in a long-term cycle lasting perhaps decades. It would seem probable that such long-fallow mixed farming formed the basis of the Fengate neolithic economy. As fen water levels rose the opportunities for seasonal exploitation of the wetlands increased. Under these circumstances it is probable that the settlement pattern tended to focus around the fen-edge, which, by the end of the third millennium BC, was probably substantially cleared of tree cover.

Fragments of polished stone axes and stray pottery sherds of the type characteristic (Grimston/Lyles Hill) of the earlier neolithic occur regularly on most subsites, either in small contemporary features, or as residual finds in features of later date. This evidence suggests that settlement was widespread, if not particularly intensive. By far and away the most important find of this period at Fengate was made on the Padholme Road subsite in the season of 1972. It was a dry season and, as water enhances soil colours, features were not showing up clearly. Very ancient features also tend to be composed of paler soil probably as a result of centuries of percolating rainwater dissolving humic material. The combination of pale soil and adverse conditions made the recognition of what we later found to be the foundation trenches of an earlier neolithic house very difficult. By a happy chance there was a short shower of rain on the freshly cleaned subsoil surface. At first nothing could be seen, but as the soil dried we could just discern, for a few hours, the faintest outlines of a rectangular structure. The ground was rapidly marked and excavation began.

Houses of the neolithic period are rare in lowland Britain and the Fengate example is therefore most significant. It measured about 7 by 8.5 metres (23 by 28 feet) and was constructed of untempered clay spread over woven wattle, the whole structure, roof and walls, being based on a wooden frame. The roof was probably thatched and the

Fig. 5 (left). A collared bead in polished jet from the earlier neolithic house, Padholme Road subsite. Length 34 mm. (Drawing by D. R. Crowther.)
Fig. 6 (right). Undecorated round-based bowl in the earlier neolithic Grimston/Lyles Hill style. From the earlier neolithic house, Padholme Road subsite. Diameter at rim 300 mm. (Drawing by D. R. Crowther.)

Plate 4. The earlier neolithic multiple burial, Cat's Water subsite. The body to the right, buried in the crouched position, had been killed by an arrowhead lodged between the eighth and ninth ribs. Scale in half metres.

charred remains of a corner post gave a radiocarbon date of 2445 BC. It is always hard to be certain about such things, but this modest building would have been suitable for housing a small family of, say, four to six people. The foundation trenches contained quantities of domestic rubbish, including Grimston/Lyles Hill pottery, numerous blade-like flint tools and waste by-products, a flake which had been detached from a polished stone axe and, finally, a remarkable jet bead. The last two finds are particularly interesting. The axe flake derived from an implement made from a rock (technically of Group VI type) whose quarry is at Langdale, Cumbria. We can only guess at how or why such an object might travel so far nearly five thousand years ago, but simple trade is unlikely to prove an adequate explanation. There are many other finds of Langdale products in the

East Midlands and some form of semi-ritualised gift exchange, which served to reinforce family ties and the like, could provide a possible explanation. The jet bead is of a type only found in neolithic contexts and is remarkable because it split in half, presumably accidentally, and was then pierced, probably with a flint borer, to convert it into a toggle. This secondary modification required two attempts before it was successfully achieved.

Following the house, the second discovery of probable neolithic date was made three years later, some 120 metres (130 yards) due east on the Cat's Water subsite. Like the house, the Cat's Water multiple burial (plate 4) was discovered by chance, during excavation of the main iron age site, discussed below. A large pit with a characteristically pale filling was found to be cut through by a late iron age ditch and on further investigation the bones of four individuals were found lying on the bottom. There was no sign of a barrow or any obvious grave marker. The bodies in this simple grave were fascinating. The most extensive remains were of a young man, aged about twenty-five, who had been buried with his legs drawn towards him, in a semi-crouched position. At his feet were the tiny bones of an infant and beyond the infant were the partially disarticulated remains of a woman, also aged about twenty-five, and a child aged about ten. The bones of the woman and child were thoroughly mixed together. Clearly one cannot be certain, but the indications are that this was a small family burial in which the woman and child appear either to have been reinterred or exposed, on some sort of platform perhaps, before final burial in the family grave. This rather sad group gains added interest by the fact that the young man had been killed by a flint arrowhead which was found lodged between his ribs.

The condition of the bones was bad, but the discovery of the arrowhead made it important that archaeologists should be able to see its location for themselves. After much effort, and with welcome help from outside, we managed to lift all the bodies, except the infant, from the ground in two large blocks of soil. These have now been consolidated in plastic and mounted on fibreglass, so that the arrowhead is in the position we found it. Both blocks are on permanent display in Peterborough Museum.

4

Phase two: expansion

The previous phase may be dated very approximately to the latter part of the third millennium BC. There is then an apparent gap of some five hundred years during which the site seems to have been abandoned. This apparent pause in occupation is not, for a number of reasons, altogether convincing, but it does coincide with the widespread flooding of the Fens that reached a peak at about 2500 BC. This semi-saltwater marine transgression laid down deposits of so-called Buttery or Fen Clay, which are, as one would expect, thicker towards the Wash, but which thin out gradually towards the western margins. We know that the Fen Clay was deposited within 6 kilometres ($3\frac{3}{4}$ miles) of the site, but it is doubtful if it could have come much closer. The extent to which this brackish water affected the local flora and fauna is hard to estimate, but it must have made some impression. Certainly the waters that laid down the clay must have drowned any fen pastures, and grazing for many years would be confined to a comparatively narrow strip of land on the margins.

These environmental changes might have affected contemporary communities in two ways. They could either adapt to the new conditions, or they could move out. On the whole, despite the lack of solid evidence to support it, the former seems the most reasonable explanation. No matter how severe the flooding, certain fen resources would still have been available and must have provided an inducement to settlement along the fen-edge. Secondly, the evidence for extensive and increasingly intensive settlement throughout and just before the second millennium BC is overwhelming and it is hard to imagine such occupation springing up unannounced, as it were. It may be suggested then that the Fen Clay marine transgression provided the stimulus to move to the flood-free gravel lands. The floods increased in intensity so that by 2500 BC, or thereabouts, settlement and grazing on the peats was impossible. Everyone now lived on flood-free land, either on the fen-edge or on islands. Pressure on land increased and gave rise, shortly before 2000 BC, to the ditched enclosure system of the late neolithic and earlier bronze ages. By this time the effects of the transgression had largely worn off and the fens were again passable in summer.

The communities of this second, expansion phase at Fengate based their economy on livestock, of which cattle seem to have been most important. Herds were grazed on the fen pastures in summer and returned to the fen-edge in winter, a pattern of seasonal movement or migration known as transhumance. Cereals were brought to the site from higher land to the west and, in the earliest phase at least, houses were probably of very light construction. The phase of expansion lasted from just before 2000 BC until about 1000 BC, when the complex system of land management evolved over the preceding millennium was suddenly abandoned.

Physical evidence for land management is provided by numerous ditches of varying depth which formed part of a system of rectilinear ditched enclosures, laid out at right angles to the fens. The main elements run northwest-southeast and parcel the land into long strips (usually separated by droveways) perhaps 50 to 150 metres wide (150-500 feet). The land in these strips is then further subdivided either into large or small enclosures or paddocks. It seems probable that the main northwest-southeast elements were laid out first and that the strips were subdivided later, according to local need. We may suppose that the strips formed the basic unit of land tenure and the pattern of development represented by the subdivisions might indicate the slightly different practices of, for example, different families.

Although the main elements of the system were often substantial, some of the smaller ditches subdividing the intervening strips of land were slight. Most of the ditches lay on lower parts of the site that had been affected to a greater or lesser extent by alluviation. The original air photographs showed the larger ditch cropmarks clearly, and their straightness and regular spacing suggested a possible Roman date.

The first season of excavation was spent developing techniques of open-area excavation, and this required that we select a spot for trial stripping where we knew archaeological features were present. The supposedly Roman trackways were ideal for this: they were straight and regularly laid out, which made their location on the ground straightforward. One simply measured their intersection with hedge lines or roads and 'joined the dots'. The first areas we cleared revealed an expanse of featureless sand-silt, some 400 millimetres ($15\frac{3}{4}$ inches) below the modern ploughsoil, which had been thickened by alluvial clays and more recent 'nightsoil' (the accumulated deposits of Peterborough's earth closets). This layer, which was about 350 millimetres ($13\frac{3}{4}$ inches) thick, was the pre-Roman topsoil. Below this it was, at last, possible to discern features clearly.

The results of our preliminary excavations were, at first, disappointing. We had expected quantities of pottery from these 'Roman trackways', but instead we found a few pieces of roughly baked cylindrical clay loomweights, scraps of soft pottery, a few lumps of fired clay with a distinctive clinker-like feel and a small, very roughly shaped bowl. There were also a few flint tools and by-products. These crude finds were patently not Romano-British, but neither were they iron age, since Abbott's researches had already produced large quantities of this pottery, with which we were, by then, familiar.

Other aspects of the supposed trackway system were peculiar, too. First, the tracks did not appear to go anywhere. Second, in at least two places, subsidiary ditches joined the main trackway ditches at right angles but were not connected to the track by gateways, as one would expect. One of these intersections produced a mass of burnt bone, charcoal and suchlike which was deposited into the ditch while it was open and in use. At another spot a well which had been dug as an enlargement of a trackway ditch produced waterlogged twigs from its lower layers. The charcoal and twigs were sent for radiocarbon dating at the end of the season. The results that came back, 1280 BC for the charcoal and 935 BC for the twigs, were most decidedly not Roman!

These first radiocarbon dates indicated that the ditch system was bronze age and not Roman; this caused us to look at the finds afresh, for they were now no longer residual items from an otherwise much later feature. The soft, hand-made potsherds were unlike other bronze age pottery from the area, but that was hardly surprising since local domestic pottery of the later second millennium BC was still virtually unknown. The flintwork was poor in quality and the few diagnostic items, such as tiny 'thumbnail' scrapers and a barbed and tanged arrowhead, all had good earlier bronze age parallels. The roughly made bowl was found alongside the clinker-like pieces of fired clay which we now know are the industrial refuse of salt manufacture. The small bowl is therefore best seen as a hastily made, disposable container or mould for salt.

Fig. 7. A highly decorated jar in the Mortlake style of the Peterborough tradition. This find came from the pre-war researches of G. W. Abbott. Diameter at rim 148 mm. (Drawing by D. R. Crowther.)

Plate 5. Vertical air photograph of the late neolithic settlement after excavation (Storey's Bar Road). The two parallel ditches at the top left of the excavated area are of Roman and late iron age date. (Photograph by S. J. Upex, Nene Valley Research Committee.)

Plate 6. The Storey's Bar Road ring-ditch during excavation (about 2000 to 1400 BC).

At first we were at a loss to explain the trackways and their associated ditches. Various ideas were suggested, some of which it is now embarrassing to recall! It eventually occurred to us that the ditches formed part of a system of land management that was laid out and in use from the beginning of the second millennium BC. The implications of this suggestion were hard to accept, even in the early 1970s. Current knowledge of bronze age land use along the fen-edge was slight, but a fully developed landscape and, perhaps more importantly, a population large enough to maintain it were decidedly unexpected developments.

We had just managed to convince ourselves that this idea could account for the existence of the 'trackways', when we began the 1973 season. Air photographs showed the Storey's Bar Road subsite was densely covered with cropmarks, many of which were probably of glacial origin. Two features were particularly clear, however. The first was a large well and the second was a ring-ditch of a type often associated with bronze age round barrows (where a circular quarry ditch was dug to provide make-up for an internal mound). Between these two features were the very faint traces of linear ditches. A large area was cleared in the hope that these disparate features might form a coherent pattern.

When the topsoil was removed the features revealed did indeed form a coherent pattern. The well was located near the edge of a ditched enclosure that formed part of a system whose alignment respected that of the trackways excavated previously. These new enclosures were defined by shallow ditches and were distinguished by entranceways sited at every available corner. A narrow ditched droveway lay alongside one enclosure and it was apparent that it had been laid out as an integral part of the original system. This narrow droveway would have been suitable for the marking or inspection of livestock.

A link with the ring-ditch was provided by the density of finds along the linear enclosure ditches, which increased gradually, but substantially, as the ring-ditch was approached. An earlier phase of the enclosure ditch originally stopped some metres short of the ring-ditch, thus forming a convenient entranceway with it. The finds distribution and the location of the early entranceway suggested that the ring-ditch and the enclosures were originally associated.

There were two areas of settlement which belonged to two different phases. The first, and earliest, was located near the well and droveway; the second was enclosed by the ring-ditch and did not extend outside it. Both areas of settlement were represented by pits and post-holes that produced considerable quantities of flint, pottery and animal bone — the usual archaeological evidence of domestic rubbish.

We were very surprised by the finds, for they could be securely dated to the late neolithic period, around 2000 BC. The pottery was highly decorated with the grooves, stabs and incisions that are characteristic of the grooved ware style. This pottery, which is peculiar to Britain, is found on many of the so called 'henge' sites of south-western England (see Aubrey Burl's *Prehistoric Stone Circles*

Fig. 8. Decorated pottery in the grooved ware style from the late neolithic settlement, Storey's Bar Road subsite. (Drawing by D. R. Crowther.)

Fig. 9. Reconstruction of the notched alder log ladder found preserved beneath the water table in the Storey's Bar Road subsite. Second millennium BC. (Drawing by D. R. Crowther).

in this series), and it was most exciting to discover a domestic site so well preserved. This discovery also raised the possibility, which we now regard as a probability, that elements (such as the main north-west-southeast droves) of the larger second millennium ditched enclosure system could have been originally laid out as early as four thousand years ago.

The settlement within the ring-ditch was abandoned and the ditch around it fell into disrepair. It would still have been visible when, at about 1460 BC, it was reused as an early bronze age burial area. The ditch was redug to slightly more than its original depth and a barrow, possibly with a turf core, was erected. Two cremations were placed in the barrow, one of which was in a very crudely made collared urn of early bronze age type. Two graves, both of children, were cut into the naturally refilling ring-ditch, probably just a few years after the erection of the barrow. A pit was excavated into the edge of the ring-ditch. This dated to the original settlement and was still open when the barrow was erected. Its lower filling was waterlogged and in it we found a remarkable notched ladder made from an alder log. The pit was probably a quarry for gravel which was spread around the settlement during winter. Presumably the ladder, which was upright when we found it, provided easy access into the pit, which by about 1000 BC had reverted to a shallow, mud-filled, stagnant pond.

By 1974 the discoveries of the previous season had whetted our appetite to learn more about the main enclosure system that we had first uncovered in 1971. Our earthmoving techniques had improved, and it was decided to place a large trial trench directly over a clearly defined element of the system on Newark Road. This preliminary trench was enlarged in the following two seasons.

Features revealed on Newark Road left us in no doubt that the ditched enclosures were part of an unusually complex land-management system of undoubted second millennium BC date. In subsequent seasons we followed the ditched enclosures eastwards, towards the Fen, on to the Fourth Drove and Cat's Water subsites, eventually linking up with the ditches we had revealed in the original excavations of 1971.

Excavating these ditches was very tedious. Enormous lengths were dug, but finds were very rarely encountered, despite the extensive use of sieving. We did, however, encounter much material suitable for radiocarbon dating and now have a series of thirty dates, spreading from about 2000 to 1000 BC. In three instances we discovered human burials which had been placed in the crouched position, without gravegoods, directly on the bottom of open ditches. These in-dividuals appear to have been buried without any archaeologically obvious ceremony or grave marking, and they should remind us that only a proportion, perhaps less than ten per cent, of the earlier bronze age population would have been buried beneath barrows.

Apart from more pottery, flint and loomweights which were similar to the examples found in 1971, we also found a fine hook or pick fashioned from the brow tine of a shed red deer antler. This im-

Fig. 10 (right). A hook or pick, possibly associated with fishing, fashioned from red deer antler. From a ditch of the second millennium system, Newark Road subsite. (Drawing by D. R. Crowther.)

Fig. 11 (below). An assortment of flints from the second millennium BC enclosure ditches of the Newark Road sub-site. From left to right: barbed and tanged arrowhead; sickle fragment; piercer or borer; scraper; core showing the scars left after the removal of flakes and blades. The scale is a cen-timetre. (Drawing by D. R. Crowther.)

Plate 7. Oblique air photograph of the second-millennium BC ditched enclosures of the Newark Road subsite during excavation. View taken looking south-east towards the junction of Padholme Road with Storey's Bar Road (left). (Photograph by S. J. Upex, Nene Valley Research Committee.)

plement could have been used for lifting fish traps or nets, as an example from a fisherman's grave in very similar contexts in the Netherlands suggests. Evidence for industrial activity included a spread of partially burnt limestone and charcoal, all from fen tree species, which (on the basis of three radiocarbon dates) had been dumped into a recut enclosure ditch at about 1000 BC. This large deposit of burnt material weighed about half a ton and is currently thought to be the remains of limeburning; but what it was used for remains a mystery. The second industrial activity for which there is good evidence is metalworking. The tip portion of a middle bronze age spearhead was found in a droveway ditch, and about 104 metres (341 feet) to the west we found a small solidified bronze drip or spill of an identical metallurgical composition. There can, therefore, be little doubt that the spearhead was manufactured at Fengate.

In 1977 we came across a remarkably well preserved length of second millennium BC ditch which had been protected from the plough by a nearby Roman road (the Fen Causeway). Beneath and to one side of the gravel road lay the ditch, but, most importantly, we also found the low, presumably hedge-capped bank which originally ran alongside it. Both ditch and bank were sealed beneath a thin deposit of flood clay which passed under the road and was therefore also of pre-Roman date. There is now evidence, elsewhere in the Fenland, for flooding at around 1000 BC. This breakdown in natural drainage, perhaps combined with a known period of climatic wetness, hastened the end of the Fengate enclosure system. By 1000 BC fen pastures were no longer available every summer and the well established pattern of transhumance, or seasonal migration into the wetlands, ceased to be viable. More reliance would be placed on an economy of mixed farming in which livestock played a less dominating role. Soon the upland and higher parts of the fen-edge would assume a more important role in this new pattern of life, which illustrates well the advantage of living at the junction of two different ecological zones.

So far we have discussed ditches rather than the people who dug and maintained them. We have seen that these people lived in small single-family units dispersed around the enclosure system and we will now briefly look at a typical house. Structure 1, Newark Road, was a round house superficially similar to the numerous examples we know from iron age contexts. The bronze age house was defined by a very shallow external eaves-drip gully which drained into an accompanying enclosure ditch. The doorway was marked by two doorposts and two smaller external porch-posts. The roof was carried on two approximately concentric rings of internal posts and there was a

Plate 8. View along the central droveway and its associated ditched enclosures, Newark Road subsite, 1974 season.

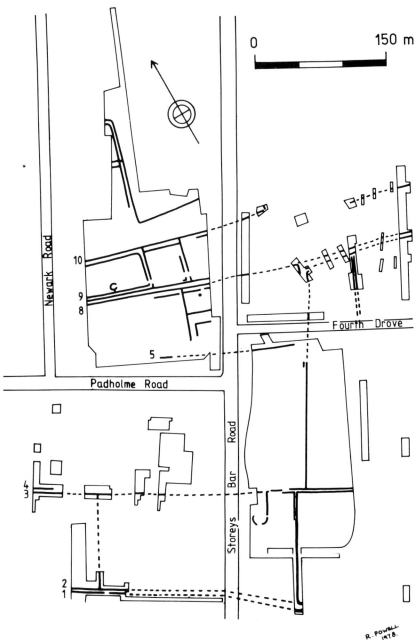

0   150 m

Newark Road

10

9
8

C

5

Fourth Drove

Padholme Road

Bar Road

Storeys

4
3

2
1

R. POWELL
1978.

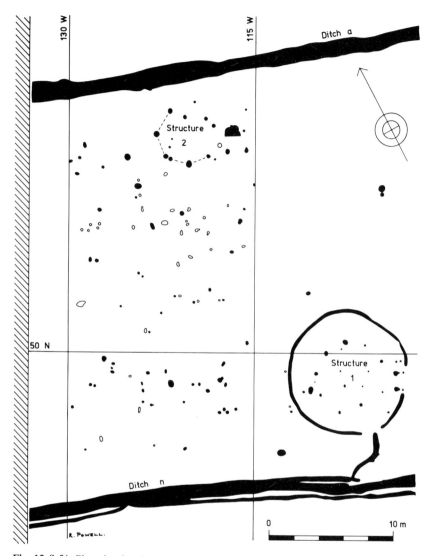

Fig. 12 (left). Plan showing the relationship of the main excavated second-millennium BC ditches.

Fig. 13 (above). Plan of second-millennium BC settlement features, Newark Road subsite. Structure 1 is a post-built round house defined by an external eaves-drip gully. Structure 2 was used to shelter livestock and has no eaves-drip gully.

hearth near the centre (evidence for which was provided by charcoal in a central post-hole). Not far from Structure 1 was a very different, simpler building — Structure 2 — which, on the evidence of the high soil phosphate concentrations nearby, was probably used to house livestock.

The settlement pattern which characterises Fengate in the second millennium BC suggests that, although the exploitation of the fen and fen-edge was intensive, settlements themselves were extensive, that is, they were spread in small units throughout the enclosure system. It would appear that single-family houses were constructed, as and when required, at any convenient spot. Despite the regular nature of the enclosure system, which might be seen as an indication of a central governing authority, the dispersed pattern of single-family settlement strongly emphasises local control. Perhaps the land was originally laid out by local agreement as part of a wider, fen-edge scheme. Subsequent evolution of the landscape would be determined by local or family needs. Archaeological evidence for a less democratic, more highly stratified society might include the construction of centralised (or *nucleated*) settlements, which will be discussed in the following chapter.

Plate 9. Rock-cut well of early iron age date (about 350 BC). Scale in half metres.

5
Phases three and four: nucleation and demise

We have seen that the previous phase of expansion came to a fairly sudden end at about 1000 BC, when communities moved and turned their attention to higher ground 'inland' from the fen. This move back from the fen was accompanied by a shift from a way of life heavily dependent on livestock to a broader-based economy centred on mixed farming. The botanical evidence for the later first millennium shows a distinct increase in weeds of cultivation, although there is still no direct evidence that cereals were grown on site.

The central social process that concerns us here is nucleation. The settlement pattern before 1000 BC was dispersed and the next phase for which there is good evidence takes place at about 300-400 BC, at the Vicarage Farm subsite. By this point settlement was nucleated and would continue to be so.

The paucity of evidence for settlement between the close of the second millennium and the middle of the first millennium BC is not a phenomenon unique to Fengate. Settlements of possible early first-millennium date might be located well back from the fen-edge, on ground above the 25-foot (7.6 metre) contour now buried beneath modern Peterborough; but this suggestion might carry more weight were other, contemporary settlements known from similar environments elsewhere. In our region, as in many other lowland areas, settlements of the early first millennium are almost as rare as those of the foregoing ten centuries; but, on the other hand, sites of the middle and later centuries are frequently encountered. On present archaeological evidence, the population of lowland Britain, as indicated by the size and number of settlements, seems to have increased quite suddenly shortly after about 500 BC. This sudden increase in population is probably more apparent than real and well illustrates the dangers of interpreting archaeological evidence too simply.

Unfortunately the estimation of past populations from archaeological data is fraught with problems. In the present case it seems that we are trying to compare two quite different types of evidence. The later, nucleated settlements of the iron age left massive archaeological traces. In the highland zone one merely has to walk across the ramparts of any reasonably sized hillfort to appreciate this. In the lowland zone, on the other hand, sites may have been flattened

Fig. 14. Early iron age handled bowl or cup from the Vicarage Farm subsite. The handle is fashioned from a wrapped wooden twig, probably of willow (about 350 BC). (Drawing by D. R. Crowther.)

by the plough, but their once enormous extent is revealed by aerial photography; as an example, although not vast, the Cat's Water iron age settlement illustrates well how nucleated settlements can create a dense and complex spread of archaeological features. By contrast, the preceding ditched enclosures of the second millennium BC were dug and maintained by a substantial population who lived in small, dispersed settlements. Their effect on the subsoil, in the form of ditches, pits and suchlike, was, by later standards, slight. On present evidence it would seem that the environmental changes of the early first millennium at Fengate were sudden in their immediate economic effect: the enclosures were rapidly abandoned and a transhumant, pastoral way of life was replaced by settled mixed farming. The principal social or cultural effect, namely settlement nucleation, which we have seen provides evidence for a stratified society, took longer to happen.

The Vicarage Farm subsite settlement represents the beginning of nucleation in the area, and it is unfortunate that its inhabitants chose to locate it upon a limestone subsoil. This bedrock, in its unweathered state, is surprisingly hard to penetrate and, although wells, pits and ditches are densely spread over the settlement area, there are no post-holes or structures. One pot found in a waterlogged deposit in the clay beneath the limestone had a remarkable wrapped wooden handle which was attached to the bowl by two small holes which had been drilled after the vessel's firing. This settlement was never, it seems, completely abandoned, but after about 300-350 BC the focus of attention moves to the Cat's Water subsite.

We have already discussed the unusual circumstances that led to the discovery of this well preserved settlement. Study of the pottery indicates that it was occupied for four distinct phases. The first possibly dates to the earlier first millennium and consists of a few isolated pits; the second (middle iron age) belongs to the second, third and even fourth centuries BC and sees the start of the main settlement. The third (late iron age) extends from the late second or early first century BC until the first half of the first century AD and is dated by the introduction and use of wheel-made pottery. The site was then abandoned for almost a century before it was briefly reoccupied, for perhaps a generation, in Roman times. The later, intermittent settlement was the result of high, fluctuating water levels and attendant fresh-water flooding which eventually led to the complete abandonment of the site. The fresh-water floods were caused by the inability of fen rivers to cope with surface water draining off the hinterland. This, in turn, was caused by obstructions, in the form of marine silts and sand bars, around the outfalls of the main Fenland rivers.

The excavation of the Cat's Water iron age settlement is important because it was sufficiently extensive to allow a full understanding of a complete settlement or series of settlements. The main settlements seem to have been occupied continuously, without significant pauses. About fifty-five possible buildings are known, of which the great ma-

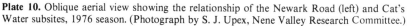

Plate 10. Oblique aerial view showing the relationship of the Newark Road (left) and Cat's Water subsites, 1976 season. (Photograph by S. J. Upex, Nene Valley Research Committee.)

Plate 11. Distant view of the Cat's Water iron age settlement during excavation, 1975 season.

jority are circular. Certain structures can undoubtedly be associated with farming, but others are less straightforwardly explained. Many round buildings, for example, showed the patterned distribution of finds on either side of the entranceway that was discussed in the Introduction. These buildings generally had low soil phosphate levels, which, taken with the patterned finds distribution, strongly suggest that they were used to house people. Buildings used to house animals over winter do not show patterned finds distributions and have high phosphate levels. It is impossible to distinguish the animal stalls from the houses simply by shape or size alone.

In general, houses were placed around the outside of the settlement, with animals nearer the centre. This was not a rigid rule, as there was also good evidence for human occupation at the centre of the settlement, but it indicates a general trend. This type of 'organic' settlement organisation contrasts with the more regimented pattern found in larger hillforts.

It seems most probable that the settlement was founded by a group of people moving to the fen-edge from higher land (perhaps from Vicarage Farm), towards the end of the fourth century BC or thereabouts. This middle iron age use of the site seems to have lasted from two hundred to three hundred years, beginning around 300 or 400 BC. Unfortunately we cannot be more precise about this date since the pottery is still poorly understood. We have seen that many of the buildings were used for sheltering livestock and the maximum possible human population was about four or five families, say twenty to twenty-five individuals, including children. This estimate is based on the last, late iron age phase of occupation, dating to about 0 BC, and it is possible that the middle iron age population may have been slightly larger, by perhaps one or two families. The middle and

Plate 12. Distant view of the Cat's Water iron age settlement (about 200 BC), 1976 season. The circular ditches define round house eaves-drip gullies.

Fig. 15. Reconstruction by Sara Lunt of part of the Cat's Water iron age settlement, about 200 BC.

late iron age phases merged into one another without a gap; the difference between the two is purely archaeological: the earlier group used hand-made pots, while the later made most of their finer wares on the potter's wheel.

Many of the ditches dug by the middle iron age community were maintained in use by the late iron age folk, so that it is often difficult to reconstruct precisely which features have early antecedents, but the evidence strongly suggests that the earlier group occupied land marginally east of the late iron age settlement area, on slightly (about 0.5 metres or 1 foot 8 inches) lower-lying land. As winter water levels continued to rise, settlement moved on to higher ground and ditches were dug deeper. The deposits that filled many of the late iron age drainage ditches contained the shells of tiny water snails of species that today live only in fresh, clear, running water. The ditch also included snails of marsh species, indicating that reeds and other vegetation were growing along the sides and bottom of the ditches. Today this vegetation will quickly block a fen dyke and must be 'slubbed out' every few years. The same must also have taken place in the iron age. This surely indicates that conditions were becoming very wet in the years immediately before and after the Roman conquest of AD 43.

The settlement contained a few burials, mainly tightly crouched within tiny, shallow graves, and there was evidence nearby for metal-working, including a unique find of a crucible fragment that had been used for melting down tin. The settlement area was transected and criss-crossed by a tangle of drainage ditches that were in sharp contrast with the straight linear enclosure ditches of the second millennium BC beneath the later features. These ditches sometimes revealed the remains of the original *brush drains* that helped to ease the flow of water away from the hamlet. One well preserved length was composed of two bundles of willow wands, cut from a coppiced or pollarded tree.

The enormous quantities of bone recovered show the usual domesticated animals, with cattle and sheep of great importance; 45 per cent of the identifiable animal bones were of cattle, 39 per cent were of sheep or goat (it is hard to distinguish between the two), 7 per cent were of horse, slightly less than 7 per cent were of pig, 2 per cent were of dog and there were three bones (0.05) per cent of cat. There was also a wealth of game, including various deer, fox and otter, and fishing was clearly important: pike, carp, bream and tench bones were recovered. Waterfowl provided an important element in the fen-edge diet in iron age times and the fare was certainly varied: greylag goose, mallard (these two may have been kept as domestic fowl),

Plate 13. Distant view of the willow brush drain, laid along the bottom of a ditch in the late iron age (about 50 BC); Cat's Water subsite. Scale in half metres.

pelican, cormorant, heron, stork, mute swan, barnacle goose, teal, tableduck, goosander, sea eagle, goshawk, buzzard, crane and coot. Iron age Fengate must have been an ornithologist's delight. The wild species, and especially the fish, indicate that local waters were fresh, or at most very slightly brackish.

We are now looking at a pattern of life which was only to alter with the widespread draining of the Fens in post-medieval times. Seventeenth-century villagers living along the fen-edge complained loudly when their fens were drained and the lush wetlands, replete with fish and fowl, were replaced by dyked fields which from time to time were devastated by catastrophic floods.

Indeed, the waters that gave prehistoric Fengate its focus soon turned. As Fenland folk have learned, the waters that provide can also destroy. Communities were pushed further back from the fen-edge and archaeological evidence for settlement is no longer found immediately east of Peterborough. But life did not stop with the passing of the Romans; the fenman in the middle ages lived an essentially iron age way of life, from which it is possible to learn much about the more remote past. We reconstruct prehistory and we should heed its archaeological lessons before the Fenland wastes away and we are left with a barren clay landscape fit only for flooding. Viewed archaeologically, the cycle that began nine thousand years ago will shortly begin again.

Plate 14 (opposite). Close-up view of the Cat's Water brush drain. The small scale (in centimetres) is placed in the gap between the two osier bundles. Large scale in half metres.

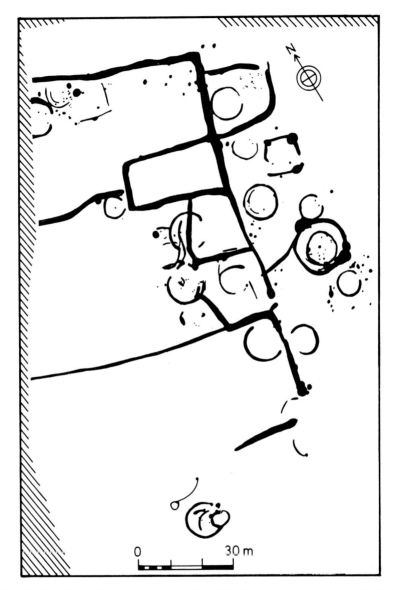

Fig. 16. Simplified outline plan of part of the middle iron age settlement on Cat's Water (300/400-100 BC). The shading indicated areas not excavated and the thick black lines are drainage ditches. Circular and semicircular gullies are eaves-drip trenches dug outside round buildings.

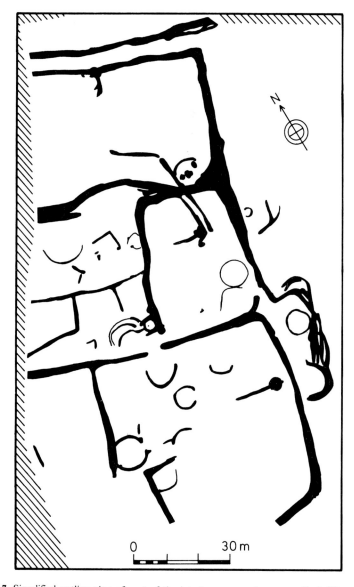

Fig. 17. Simplified outline plan of part of the late iron age settlement on Cat's Water (100 BC to AD 50/60). Note the slight movement of buildings westwards, on to higher ground, as water levels rose. Note also the rarity of small pits and post-holes, since wood would rot quickly in such conditions.

Plate 15. A ground-level view of two buildings of the Cat's Water middle iron age settlement (about 200 BC). (Model made by Eric Ricketts and David Rayner; model and photograph courtesy of Peterborough Development Corporation.)

Plate 16. Towards the end of the project factory building was fast encroaching on the land released by the archaeologists. The dark building in the background was placed over the ditched fields of the Newark Road subsite, while the earlier neolithic house lies below the factory whose roof is visible at the extreme left of the picture. The circular ditch and associated gullies in the foreground form the southern edge of the Cat's Water later iron age settlement and probably represent the remains of an animal byre and its connected yards.

Further reading

Fen, fen-edge and wetlands
The following sources all have comprehensive bibliographies from which it should be possible to obtain further references.

Godwin, H. *Fenland: its Ancient Past and Uncertain Future*. Cambridge University Press, 1978.

Coles, J. M. and Orme, B. J. *Prehistory of the Somerset Levels*. Somerset Levels Project, Cambridge and Exeter, 1980.

Phillips, C. W. (editor). *The Fenland in Roman Times*. Royal Geographical Society Research Series number 5, 1970. A most important collection of essays, of special relevance to the 'silt fens' around the Wash.

Royal Commission on Historical Monuments (England). *A Matter of Time: an Archaeological Survey*. HMSO, London, 1960. The original and still definitive account of river gravel sites; of special importance to the Welland valley immediately north of Fengate.

Thompson, F. H. (editor). *Archaeology and Coastal Change*. Society of Antiquaries Occasional Paper (new series) number 1, London, 1980. An authoritative and up-to-date account of recent work; the papers by Simmons, Devoy and Louwe Kooijmans are particularly relevant to East Anglia.

Wild, J. P. 'Roman Settlement in the Lower Nene Valley'. *Archaeological Journal* 131, pages 140-70, 1974. A comprehensive synthesis, mainly devoted to land west of Peterborough.

Fengate, the site (previous research)
Abbott, G. W. 'The Discovery of Prehistoric Pits at Peterborough'. *Archaeologia* 62, pages 332-52, 1910. The first account of Fengate by its discoverer, with an important contribution by Reginald Smith.

Hawkes, C. F. C. and Fell, C. I. 'The Early Iron Age Settlement at Fengate, Peterborough'. *Archaeological Journal* 100, pages 188-223, 1945. The third paper on Abbott's discoveries.

Leeds, E. T. 'Further Discoveries of the Neolithic and Bronze Ages at Peterborough'. *Antiquaries Journal* 2, pages 220-37, 1922. The second paper on Abbott's discoveries.

Mahany, C. M. 'Fengate'. *Current Archaeology* 17, pages 156-7, 1969. An interim account of a rather enigmatic neolithic or bronze age site excavated in 1968.

Fengate, the site (the recent project)

The first two reports are published by the Royal Ontario Museum, Toronto, and may be obtained direct from Canada or from the Nene Valley Research Committee, Ham Lane House, Orton Waterville, Peterborough, PE2 0UU. The First Report is mainly devoted to the earlier neolithic house and the Second Report considers the late neolithic enclosures of the Storey's Bar Road subsite.

The Third Report is jointly published by the Royal Ontario Museum and the Northamptonshire Archaeological Society and is obtainable from the society's editor, A. E. Brown, Department of Adult Education, The University, Leicester, LE1 7RH. The Third Report considers the ditched enclosure system of the second millennium BC. The Fourth Report will be obtainable from the same source as the Third and should appear in 1982. This, the final report, is mainly concerned with the Cat's Water iron age settlement, but it also includes a discussion of the other periods represented at Fengate and places them in their wider contexts.

Pryor, F. M. M. 'A Neolithic Multiple Burial from Fengate, Peterborough'. *Antiquity* 50, pages 232-3, 1976. This burial is fully described in chapter 4 of the Fourth Report.

Pryor, F. M. M. 'Raising the Fengate Dead'. *Durobivae* 8, pages 15-18, 1980. An illustrated account of the block-lifting of the neolithic multiple burial.

Pryor, F. M. M. 'Will It All Come Out in the Wash? Reflections at the End of Eight Years' Digging' in J. Barrett and R. J. Bradley (editors) *Settlement and Society in the British Later Bronze Age,* pages 483-500. British Archaeological Reports, 83, Oxford, 1980. A candid assessment of Fengate with thoughts on future research.

Pryor, F. M. M. and Cranstone, D. A. L. 'An Interim Report on Excavations at Fengate, Peterborough, 1975-77'. *Northamptonshire Archaeology* 13, pages 9-27, 1978. A full interim report, with plans, of the Cat's Water iron age settlement.

Index

Page numbers in italics refer to illustrations

Peterborough New Town 5, 6
Peterborough pottery 6, *25*
Phosphate analysis 10-12, 40
Plough damage 9, 38
Radiocarbon dates 5, 21, 25, 30
Ring-ditch, neolithic *26, 27,* 28
Romano-British settlement 39,
  44
Saltern debris 25
Seasonality 17, 19, 23, 32
Shippea Hill 13, 19

Smith, Reginald 6
Snails 44
Social structure 36, 41
Spearhead, bronze 36
Storey's Bar Road subsite *8,*
  *26*ff
Taylor, Maisie 14
Transhumance 32
Vicarage Farm subsite *8,* 37ff
Welland valley, sites 5
Wells, 'sock' 6, 25, 27-8